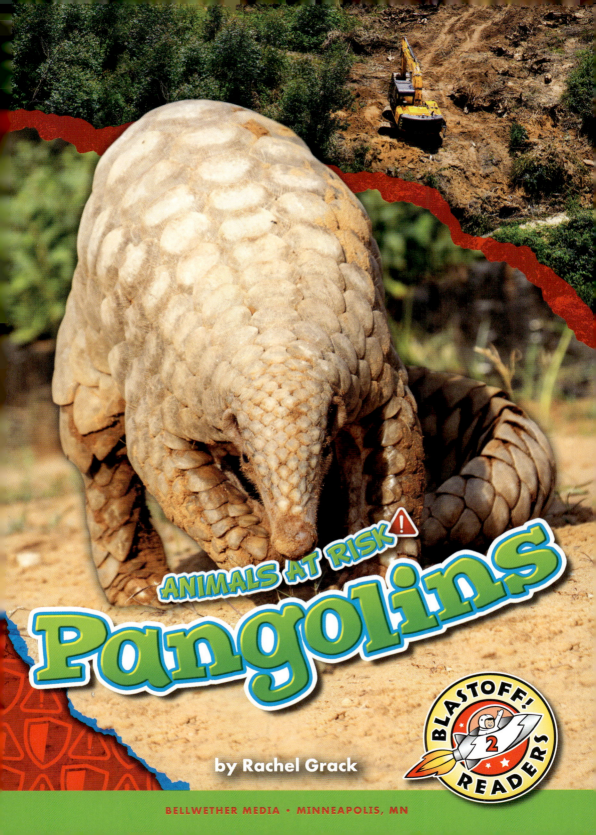

ANIMALS AT RISK
Pangolins

by Rachel Grack

BLASTOFF! READERS 2

BELLWETHER MEDIA • MINNEAPOLIS, MN

Blastoff! Readers are carefully developed by literacy experts to build reading stamina and move students toward fluency by combining standards-based content with developmentally appropriate text.

LEVELS

 Level 1 provides the most support through repetition of high-frequency words, light text, predictable sentence patterns, and strong visual support.

 Level 2 offers early readers a bit more challenge through varied sentences, increased text load, and text-supportive special features.

 Level 3 advances early-fluent readers toward fluency through increased text load, less reliance on photos, advancing concepts, longer sentences, and more complex special features.

★ **Blastoff! Universe**

Reading Level

 Grade K  Grades 1–3  Grade 4

This edition first published in 2025 by Bellwether Media, Inc.

No part of this publication may be reproduced in whole or in part without written permission of the publisher. For information regarding permission, write to Bellwether Media, Inc., Attention: Permissions Department, 6012 Blue Circle Drive, Minnetonka, MN 55343.

Library of Congress Cataloging-in-Publication Data

LC record for Pangolins available at: https://lccn.loc.gov/2024009421

Text copyright © 2025 by Bellwether Media, Inc. BLASTOFF! READERS and associated logos are trademarks and/or registered trademarks of Bellwether Media, Inc. Bellwether Media is a division of Chrysalis Education Group.

Editor: Kieran Downs   Designer: Brittany McIntosh

Printed in the United States of America, North Mankato, MN.

Table of Contents

Scaly Animals 4
In Danger! 8
Save the Pangolins! 12
Glossary 22
To Learn More 23
Index 24

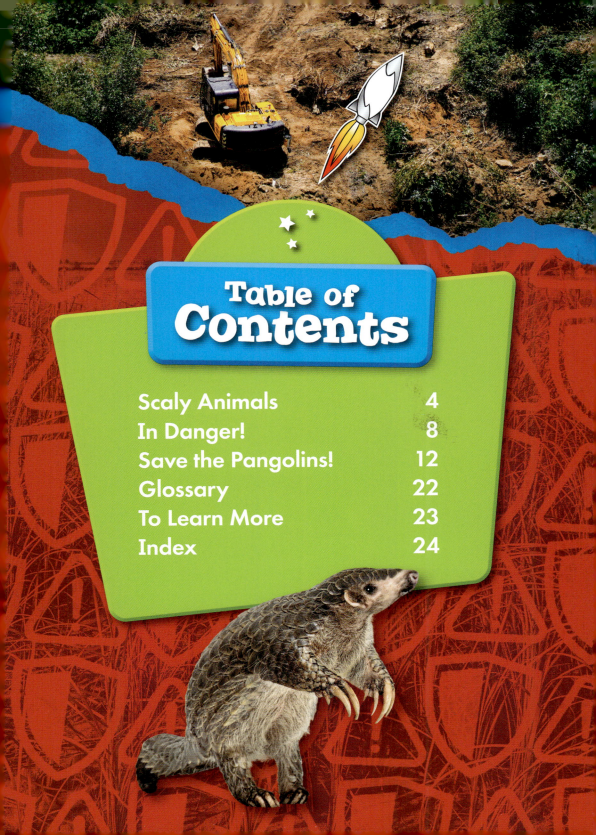

Scaly Animals

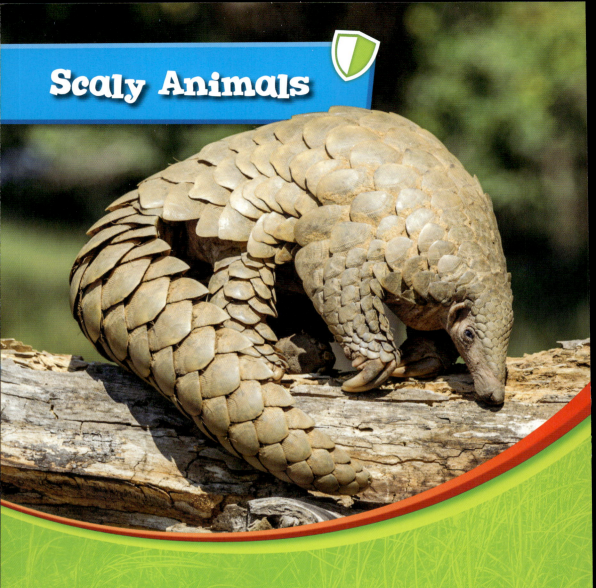

Pangolins are **mammals** with **scales**. They have sharp claws. They eat **insects** with their long tongues.

There are eight **species**. They live in Africa and Asia.

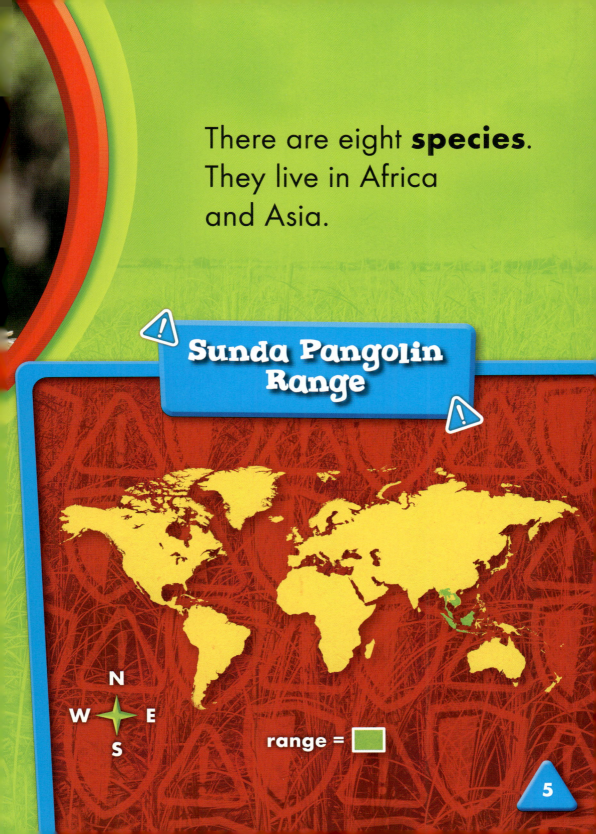

Sunda Pangolin Range

range =

Pangolins once filled forests and **grasslands**. But their numbers are dropping. Some species are **critically endangered**.

People have caused most of their problems.

In Danger!

People hunt pangolins. They use their scales in medicines. They also make jewelry.

Some people eat their meat.

scales

Sunda Pangolin Stats

conservation status: critically endangered
life span: up to 7 years

logging

Pangolin homes are getting smaller. People clear land for farms. They cut down forests for **logging**.

Farm **pesticides** kill insects. Pangolins have less food.

Threats

1. people need farms
2. people clear land
3. pangolins lose their homes

Save the Pangolins!

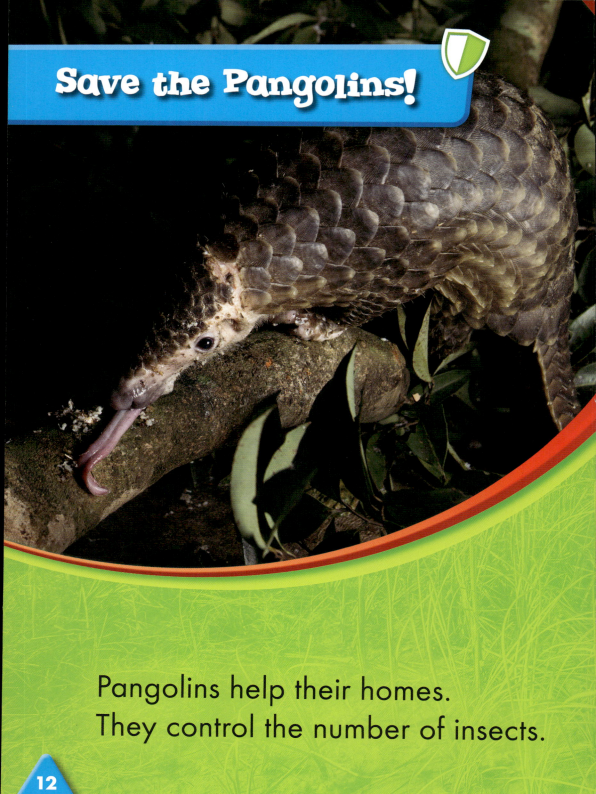

Pangolins help their homes.
They control the number of insects.

They dig up the ground to find food. This keeps the soil healthy.

The World with Pangolins

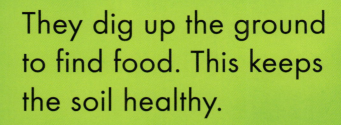

1. more pangolins

2. healthy soil

3. healthy forests and grasslands

Governments pass **laws** to help pangolins.
It is illegal to hunt them.

Police work to stop hunters.

Farmers learn new ways to grow crops. They use less land. Fewer trees are cut down. Grasslands go untouched.

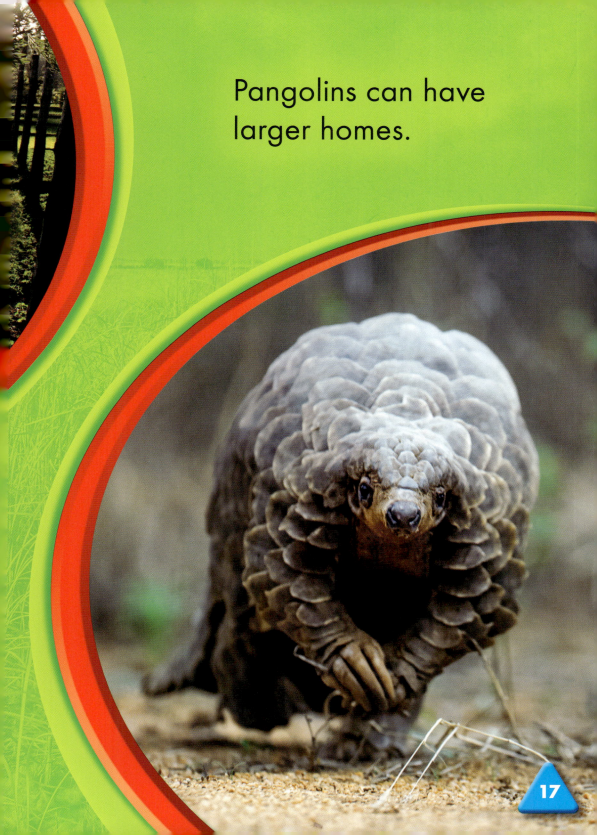

Pangolins can have larger homes.

Wildlife workers move pangolins to **reserves**. They use **technology** to track them.

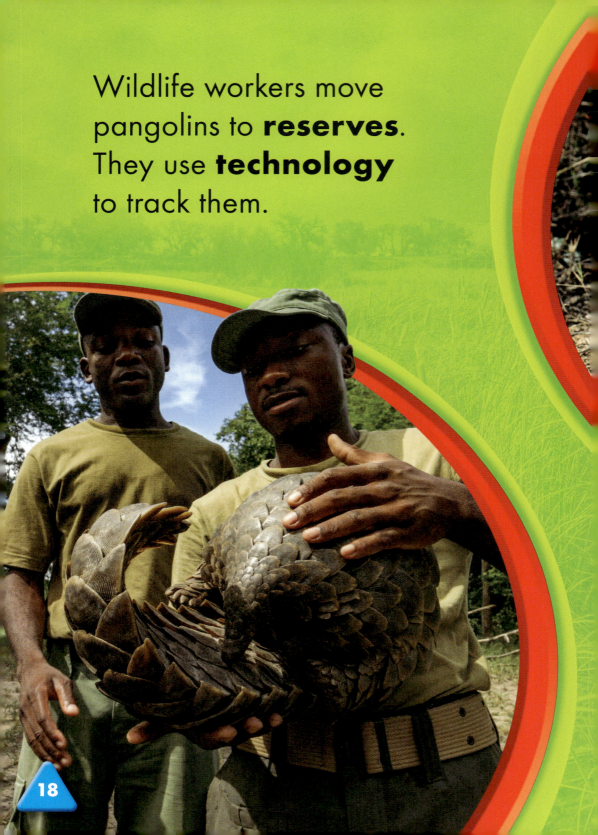

The animals stay safe and healthy.

Donations help wildlife workers care for pangolins. Telling others about illegal hunting can help.

Adopting a pangolin also helps. Everyone can save these scaly animals!

Glossary

adopting—taking over the care for someone or something; people who adopt wild animals give money for someone else to care for them.

critically endangered—greatly in danger of dying out

donations—gifts for a certain cause; most donations are money.

grasslands—lands covered with grasses and other soft plants with few bushes or trees

insects—small animals with six legs and bodies divided into three parts

laws—rules that must be followed

logging—cutting and moving trees for timber

mammals—warm-blooded animals that have backbones and feed their young milk

pesticides—materials that kill pests such as insects or weeds

reserves—lands set aside for wildlife

scales—small plates that cover an animal's body

species—kinds of animals

technology—tools created by science used to make and share useful things or to solve problems

To Learn More

AT THE LIBRARY

Culliford, Amy. *Pangolin*. New York, N.Y.: Crabtree Publishing, 2024.

Jaycox, Jaclyn. *Pangolins*. North Mankato, Minn.: Pebble, 2022.

Willis, John. *Pangolins*. New York, N.Y.: Lightbox Learning, 2023.

ON THE WEB

Factsurfer.com gives you a safe, fun way to find more information.

1. Go to www.factsurfer.com.

2. Enter "pangolins" into the search box and click 🔍.

3. Select your book cover to see a list of related content.

Index

Africa, 5
Asia, 5
claws, 4
critically endangered, 6
crops, 16
donations, 20
farmers, 16
farms, 10, 11
food, 11, 13
forests, 6, 10
governments, 14
grasslands, 6, 16
homes, 10, 12, 17
hunt, 8, 14, 15, 20
insects, 4, 11, 12
land, 10, 16
laws, 14
logging, 10
mammals, 4
meat, 8
numbers, 6
people, 7, 8, 10
pesticides, 11

police, 15
range, 5
reserves, 18
scales, 4, 8, 20
soil, 13
species, 5, 6
stats, 9
technology, 18
threats, 11
tongues, 4
trees, 16
ways to help, 20
wildlife workers, 18, 20
world with, 13

The images in this book are reproduced through the courtesy of: Vickey Chauhan, front cover, pp. 11 (bottom), 20-21; Jishith Jayaram, front cover (tear), p. 3; Eric Isselee, p. 3; Nature Picture Library/ Alamy, p. 4; paula french, p. 6; Hemis/ Alamy, p. 7; Nick Greaves, p. 8; Ari Asp999, pp. 8-9, 14; Fabian Plock, p. 10; PradeepGaurs, p. 11 (left); Santhosh Varghese, p. 11 (right); Suzi Eszterhas/ Wild Wonders of China, pp. 12, 20; Robin Bruyns, p. 13 (left); imageBROKER.com GmbH & Co. KG/ Alamy, p. 13 (right); Icswart, p. 13 (bottom); Eugene Troskie, p. 15; Chess Ocampo, p. 16; Neil Aldridge, p. 17; Jen Guyton, p. 18; SuperStock/ Roland Seitre/ Minden Pictures, p. 19; dwi putra stock, p. 23.